puppy care & training

understanding and
caring for your pet

Written by
Julia Barnes

magnet
& steel

Magnet & Steel Ltd

www.magnetsteel.com

ISBN: 978-1-907337-13-0
ISBN: 1-907337-13-X

Contents

Introduction

Introduction

Owning a dog is a hugely rewarding and enriching experience, so there is little wonder that it is one of the most popular of all pets, ranking only below the cat.

There are good reasons for why cats come top in the popularity stakes. Dogs offer qualities of love, loyalty and companionship, which you are unlikely to find in the independent-minded cat, but a dog does require a lot more time and attention, which means he is not the perfect pet for everyone.

If you decide to take on a dog, life will never be the same – which has both positive and negative connotations. You are responsible for his care in terms of providing the correct diet, attending to his grooming requirements, and giving him sufficient exercise. But of equal importance is the need to give your dog time.

A dog thrives on human companionship and he will be miserable – and even destructive – if he is kept on his own for long periods.

You will need to organise your day so you spend time with your dog and give him the attention he deserves. If you go out to work, this will involve making special arrangements so your dog is never left 'home alone' for longer than four hours at a stretch.

Yes, it is a big commitment. But in return a dog will be your devoted companion, a non-judgemental friend who is always thrilled to see you, and wants nothing more than to be at your side. If you take the big step of bringing a dog into your home, make sure you keep your half of the bargain – and it will be a decision you never regret.

Discovering dogs

Regardless of whether you own a tiny Chihuahua or an enormous Great Dane, all dogs share a common ancestor. They are all descended from the wolf, and even though dogs have been domesticated for more than 14,000 years, we can still see wolf-like behaviour in our pets.

In the wild, the wolf is a pack animal, which means he lives in a tightly-knit unit and abides by the rules of the pack leaders. The top-ranking male and female – the alpha male and alpha female – are the decision-makers. The other members of the pack, who are all closely related, occupy different places in the hierarchy depending on their age and status.

The lower-ranking members of the pack accept the leaders' authority because this constitutes their best chance of survival. Instead of being a lone animal hunting on his own, and trying to fend off attacks from enemies, a wolf living in a pack enjoys the protection of high-ranking leaders, and the chances of hunting success are vastly increased when working as a team member.

Despite thousands of years of domestication, our pet dogs still retain all the instincts of pack animals. A dog is highly sociable and is willing to co-operate with, and accept the leadership that is offered to him in his human pack. You must be prepared to take on this role, providing food, housing and protection, and teaching him the behaviour you want so that he becomes a fully integrated member of your family circle.

Development of dog breeds

There are over 400 different breeds of dog worldwide showing such diversity of size, coat and colour that it is hard to believe they can all be traced back to one common ancestor. How did the different breeds develop and what was the reason for it?

The first wolves that lived alongside humans proved their worth as hunters, helping their masters to track prey, to bring it down, and then to bring it home. Their other duty was to guard the home, warning the family if strangers were approaching.

As civilisation developed, farming became increasingly important, and, again, the now domesticated dogs were able to help, herding the livestock and protecting it from predators.

Centuries later, the ladies of the aristocracy wanted pretty, little lap dogs that could be played with and cuddled.

So it was, that different dogs were developed for different jobs. Big, impressive looking dogs were used for guarding, dogs with good scenting ability were required for hunting, quick, clever, agile dogs worked with livestock, and dainty little dogs became sweet-tempered companions. The males and females that showed the best ability in their specialist field were bred together to produce puppies that would be built for the job. They would replicate their parents' temperament and working skills. In this way, breed type was gradually established and became fixed over succeeding generations.

The main groups

Dog breeds are divided into seven main groups, which relate to their original working function.

Hounds

These are the dogs that were bred for hunting, using their scenting ability or eyesight to hunt prey. Hounds are divided into two smaller groups – sighthounds and scent hounds.

Scenthounds come in all shapes and sizes from the lofty Irish Wolfhound to the long, low, Dachshund. The Bloodhound and the Basset Hound are highly recognisable members of this group.

Sighthounds are fast-moving and athletic, and tend to share an elegance in appearance. They include the Greyhound, the fastest dog in the world, the Afghan Hound with his long, flowing coat, and the Basenji, a hunting dog from Africa.

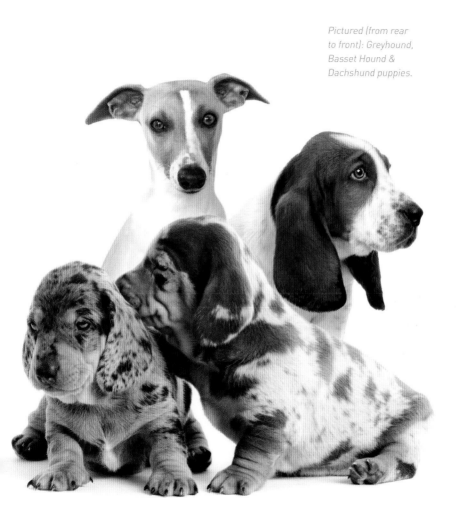

Gundogs/ sporting

These are all the breeds that were bred to help on shoots; tracking and retrieving game shot by the gun.

They include Retrievers who would find fallen game on land and in water and carry it in their soft mouths back to their master. Labradors, Goldens and Curly Coats are all popular representatives of this group.

Spaniels, such as the Cocker, the English Springer and the Welsh Springer were used to hunt and flush out game from thick undergrowth. Setters, such as the striking, red Irish and the black and tan Gordon Setter, were used to find and set game for the guns, while the Pointer showed an unusual talent for indicating game by freezing on point.

The multi-talented European gundogs were bred to hunt, point and retrieve and they include the German Shorthaired Pointer and the Italian Spinone.

Pictured (clockwise from top): English Springer Spaniel, Golden Retriever, Chocolate Labrador & Cocker Spaniel puppies.

Pastoral

The dogs that were bred to herd and protect livestock – both sheep and cattle – come into this category. They include all the Collie breeds, such as the Border Collie, the Bearded Collie and the Rough Collie, as well as the German Shepherd Dog, the Australian Cattle Dog and the diminutive Corgi.

Pictured (from left):
German Shepherd, Border
Collie, Corgi & Bearded
Collie puppies.

Working

The big, powerful guard dogs are in this group. They include the canine heavyweights such as the Mastiff, the Bullmastiff and the Dogue de Bordeaux. The Nordic sled dogs, such as the Siberian Husky and the Alaskan Malamute, are also placed in the Working group.

Pictured (from left):
Mastiff & Siberian Husky
puppies.

Terriers

Big on personality, these feisty, courageous dogs were bred to kill vermin, such as rats, and to go to ground after fox and badger. They include the ever-popular Jack Russell, the West Highland White, and the Border Terrier. In the 18th century dogs were used for fighting, and breeds such as the Staffordshire Bull Terrier and the Bull Terrier evolved. Thankfully, this sport has long since died out, and these breeds are now much-loved companion dogs.

Pictured (from left): Border Terrier, Jack Russell & West Highland White Terrier puppies.

Utility/non sporting

This is a group where anything goes – most of the breeds have a working past, but they were all used for different purposes. There is the Dalmatian which used to run alongside horse-drawn carriages, the Tibetan breeds, such as the Lhasa Apso and the Shih Tzu which were temple dogs, and the Poodle, which comes in Standard, Miniature and Toy sizes.

Toy

Bred to be lap dogs for the nobility, Toy dogs have often been the favourites of royalty. They include the Cavalier King Charles Spaniel, the Pekingese, the Chihuahua, and the Bichon Frise. The Yorkshire Terrier – with its glamorous long coat– is also included, although the breed was originally known for its excellent ratting abilities!

Understanding dogs

"My dog understands every word I say..." You may well have heard a devoted owner talk about his dog in this way, ¬ but how true is it? Dogs are good at tuning into human feelings and they are very clever at reading our body language, but we should also make some effort to understand our dogs and see the world through their eyes.

The senses

The dog is primarily designed to be a hunter, and his senses are finely tuned to give him the best possible chance of success.

Eyesight

Most dogs' eyes are set wide apart which gives the best field of vision. They are very good at picking up the slightest movement – even from a distance – but are less able to focus on detail. Dogs see better than people in the dark, but they are not so sensitive to colours. It is thought that dogs see in a range of purples, violets and yellows.

Scenting ability

Dogs have an amazing sense of smell – about one thousand times better than a human's. Dogs use their scenting ability to follow tracks of other animals, and also to pick up information from other dogs that have passed through the area and left their mark by urinating or defecating.

Hearing

Dogs have a superior sense of hearing and can pick up sounds that are four times further away than we can. Dogs can use one ear at a time or both at the same time.

Body language

Dogs come in all shapes and sizes, and can look radically different from each other. Some have erect ears, some have ears that fall by the side of their heads, some have long tails, some have tails curled over their backs, some have long coats, some have short coats, and some have curly coats.

However, dogs see past these differences and read body language so they understand what another dog is communicating. This is one of the reasons why it is so important to socialise a puppy with other dogs so that he learns the art of canine communication.

- A confident, happy dog will have a relaxed body posture, a calm expression and a wagging tail.

- A worried dog will have a crouched body posture with ears back and tail down.

- An assertive dog will stand tall, with tail held high, and a keen, alert expression.

- A dog may raise his hackles (the hair along his back) to look as scary as possible. Some dogs may be showing aggression, but others are apprehensive.

- A playful dog will go into the bow position which shows he is inviting another dog to play.

- An aggressive dog will stand tall, freeze, and maybe curl back his upper lip in a snarl.

Verbal communication

Dogs communicate by using a range of different sounds, which include the following:

Whimpering

A puppy may whimper when he is cold or hungry as a signal to his mother. A puppy settling in a new home may also do this.

Barking

This is sometimes used as a warning, often at the approach of strangers. Some dogs bark when they are excited, or it could be a sign of frustration.

Whining

Generally a sign of discomfort, but some dogs will whine to get attention.

Growling

This is an important warning signal, meaning: "If you do not take heed, worse will follow".

Howling

It is thought that wolves howl as a means of distant communication, and it also used as a bonding exercise among pack members. In domestic dogs, it may be triggered by an unusual sound, or by hearing other dogs barking.

Making the decision

Before you take the major step of buying a puppy, weigh up the pros and cons so you are 100 per cent confident that a dog will fit into your lifestyle.

Pros

- A puppy will grow into a loving companion and will become part of your family.

- There are considerable health benefits to owning a dog. You will get regular exercise, and there is therapeutic value from stroking and caring for a dog.

- If you have children, you can teach valuable lessons in taking responsibility for a dog and establishing mutual respect.

Cons

- Regardless of his age, a dog should not be left on his own for more than four hours a day, so if you go out to work you will need to make suitable dog-sitting arrangements. A puppy cannot be left for this long as it is important to establish a house-training routine at an early age.

- If you want to go on holiday, you will have to make arrangements for your dog if you do not want to take him with you.

- There are financial implications involved in owning a dog, which go beyond the purchase price of a puppy. You need to budget for food, grooming expenses if you have a high maintenance breed, routine preventative health care (e.g. vaccinations, flea and worming treatment), vet bills for unexpected problems, pet-sitting and possibly fees for boarding kennels.

- You will need to exercise your dog on a daily basis – regardless of the weather!

- If you are house-proud, you may struggle as even the best cared for dogs shed hairs on the carpet and come home from a walk with muddy paws.

- Some dogs are keen gardeners – though not in a way you would appreciate! If you own a dog, the lawn will suffer in places where he urinates, and you may have to guard against attempts to tunnel to Australia.

- A puppy needs a comprehensive programme of training and socialisation in order to become a confident, well-balanced canine citizen. You need to find the time for regular training sessions as well as going on outings to socialise your pup.

- In the first few weeks, you will need to spend time house-training your puppy – and this also means clearing up the occasional 'accident'.

As you can see, there are plenty of practical reasons why dog ownership will not suit everyone. However, dog lovers agree that the rewards far outweigh any negative considerations. But it is important that you are in possession of all the facts before you bring a puppy into your home.

Choosing a breed

What breed of dog will best suit your family and lifestyle? There are a number of factors to bear in mind when choosing the perfect pet.

Inherited behaviour

The first, and most important consideration is to find out the background of a breed and the reason why that breed was developed. This will give you a very good indication of temperament and behavioural traits. For example, a breed such as the Border Collie that was bred to herd sheep retains strong working instincts and therefore needs both physical exercise and mental stimulation. In contrast, a Toy breed such as a Cavalier King Charles Spaniel was bred to be the perfect companion and wants nothing more than to be with his beloved family.

Size

This may be obvious, but you need to work out how big, or how small, a dog is right for you. If you fancy a giant breed, such as a Mastiff or a St. Bernard, you need enough space in your home, and in your car. You should also take into account that large breeds will be more expensive to feed. Small breeds, such as a Pug or a Dachshund, are very adaptable and will take to apartment dwelling, which may be a consideration if you live in a city.

Coat

For some people grooming a dog is a pleasurable occupation, for others it is simply a chore. No matter how much you like the look of a breed, bear in mind the workload involved in keeping the coat in good order. A longcoated breed, such as the Afghan Hound, will need daily grooming, whereas a shortcoated breed like a Labrador Retriever needs little more than a weekly brush. Some breeds, such as the Poodle and many of the terrier breeds, need regular trips to the grooming parlour, which is an expense to consider. If you want a longcoated breed, such as a Shih Tzu, but you cannot cope with the grooming, you can consider keeping your dog in pet trim, which looks smart and is easy to maintain.

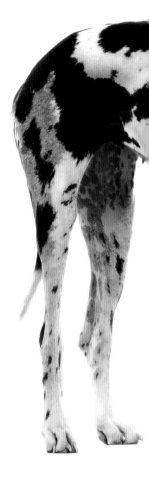

Exercise

All breeds of dog need some exercise, which should be combined with mental stimulation, such as taking your dog to a new place or playing a favourite game with him. However, you can also choose your breed depending on how much exercise you enjoy. Sporting breeds, such as Spaniels and Retrievers are energetic, exuberant dogs who love to be busy investigating new sights and smells. The Working and Pastoral breeds, such as the Collie breeds, also thrive on plenty of exercise. Generally speaking, smaller breeds need less exercise, but do not let your dog turn into a pampered pooch who becomes fat and unhealthy because he spends his life on the sofa.

Training

In order to be a well-behaved canine citizen, your dog will need to attain a basic level of training and undergo a programme of socialisation so that he will be happy and confident in all situations. For some owners, interest in training stops there; others are keen to reach higher standards and get involved in one of the canine sports, such as Competitive Obedience or Agility. All dogs can be trained to an advanced level – but some are definitely easier than others! The breeds that have been developed to work closely with people, such as the Sporting and Working breeds, are generally more biddable; hounds and terriers have a tendency to follow their own agenda...

If you have not owned a dog before and are new to training, do not be too ambitious. Some breeds such as German Shepherd Dogs, Rottweilers and Dobermanns are wonderful dogs, but they do need an experienced handler.

Life expectancy

Unfortunately dogs have a far shorter life span
than we do. On average, a dog will live to 12 years,
although many live considerably longer. The Toy
breeds have the best life expectancy and may survive
well into their teens. The giant breeds are not long
lived, and it is very rare for a Great Dane, for example,
to reach double figures.

Crossbreeds/ mongrels

A crossbreed refers to a dog that has different
pedigree parents, such as a Labrador Retriever
and a Poodle, creating a Labradoodle, which has
become a popular choice in recent times. If a dog
has no known pedigree ancestry, he is referred to as
a mongrel. These dogs make great family pets, but if
you buy a puppy, you will have no idea how big he will
grow or what his temperament will be like.

Finding a puppy

Once you have decided on the breed to suit your family and lifestyle, the next step is to find a litter of puppies. With internet access, this is not difficult, but how do you know you are contacting a reputable breeder who produces sound, healthy puppies that are typical of the breed?

The best plan is to go to a recommended source. The easiest way to do this is to contact the Kennel Club – the governing body of pedigree dog registrations and activities – and get contact details for Breed Clubs in your area. The Breed Club secretary can give you details of local breeders and may know who has puppies available.

The other route you can take is to visit a dog show where the breed of your choice is scheduled. If you go to a Championship Show you will see some of the best dogs in the country and you will be able to work out what type and colour you like best. When judging is over, you can talk to the exhibitors of the dogs, and they will be able to tell you of their breeding plans as well as giving useful advice.

Bear in mind that you may have to wait some time before you can buy the puppy of your dreams. Most breeders only plan a litter once or twice a year, and many will have a waiting list of prospective puppy buyers.

Male or female?

Before you go to see a litter, it will be helpful if you have made up your mind as to whether you want a male (dog) or a female (bitch). Every dog is an individual and so it is impossible to generalise about the temperament of either sex. However, there are a few points to consider:

- In most breeds, the male will be bigger and stronger than the female. This does not apply to Toy breeds where males and females are about the same size.

- If you are opting for one of the more challenging breeds – a Rottweiler or a Boxer, for example – the male may be more assertive and will require firm handling.

- A female will come into season every six to nine months, and during this three-week period she must be kept away from entire (un-neutered) males to avoid the risk of an unwanted pregnancy.

- A male that is not neutered will have a one-track mind when it comes to females. He will be on the lookout for bitches in season, and he will be keen to mark (cock his leg) so he can signal to other males and females in the area.

- If you already have a dog, you will need to choose the sex which is most likely to be compatible. Ask the breeder for advice as compatibility between the sexes may vary from breed to breed.

If you do not plan to get involved in breeding, the best course of action is to neuter your dog, which has many health benefits as well as simplifying dog management. You vet will give further advice, and will also recommend the most suitable age for carrying out this procedure.

Colour?

There are some breeds, such as the Bichon Frise, which is pure white, and you will have no choice of colour. But most breeds come in a variety of colours, and may have different markings. There are some breeds, such as the Golden Retriever, that come in one colour but you can choose any shade from the deepest red to the palest cream. Some colours are less common, and if you opt for rarity value, you may have longer to wait for your puppy.

More Than One?

You may decide that you want two dogs in your life so that they can be company for each other. This can work well, but resist the temptation to buy two puppies from the same litter – no matter how appealing the pups look when they are playing together! Pups of the same age will bond with each other rather than with their human family, and unless you can guarantee that you can give each puppy lots of individual training and attention, you will regret your decision. Ideally, wait until your dog is around two years old before taking on another.

Assessing the litter

Who can resist an adorable puppy? You would need a heart of stone to turn your back on a litter of pups, but this is a time when you must keep a cool head. You are taking on a dog for the duration of his life, and you do not want to face possible heartbreak by buying a sickly or unsuitable puppy.

Look for the following signs of a healthy, well-reared litter:

- The environment where the puppies are kept should be clean and smell fresh.

- The puppies should come running to greet you, and they should be lively and playful.

- The pups should be well covered but not pot-bellied, which could indicate the presence of roundworm.

- Eyes should be bright and free from discharge; ears should be clean and free from odour, noses should be free from discharge with no sign of crustiness.

- Coats should be clean and free from dandruff. Evidence of matting around the rear end could indicate diarrhoea.

Watch the puppies playing together to get an idea of their individual personalities, and also ask to see the mother of the puppies so you can see the temperament they are likely to inherit.

If you are planning to exhibit your dog in the show ring, make sure you inform the breeder so you can assess show potential. There is no guarantee of success, but the breeder can help you to evaluate conformation, movement and other important breed characteristics.

The breeder will have spent many hours 'puppy watching' and will have a good knowledge of each puppy in the litter. Discuss your family set-up and lifestyle and the breeder will help you to pick out the perfect pup.

Getting ready

In most cases, a breeder will not allow puppies to go to their new homes until they are eight weeks old. In the case of small Toy breeds, they will not be ready to go until they are at least 12 weeks old. However, there is plenty to get ready before the big day arrives.

In the home

An inquisitive puppy will want to explore every nook and cranny of his new home, so you need to make sure the environment is free from potential hazards. A puppy will investigate everything with his mouth which can be lethal; he can jump up and pull things on top of him; he can get stuck in the smallest corner, and he can move with surprising speed if a door is left open.

Look at your home from your puppy's perspective and try to eliminate possible danger:

- Tidy all electric cables so they are well out of reach.

- Check fastenings on all ground-floor cupboards, particularly where cleaners/disinfectants are kept.

- Move valuable/breakable objects from coffee tables or other surfaces where a puppy could reach.

- If you have children, make sure toys are stored safely; many accidents have resulted from a puppy chewing and swallowing an unsuitable toy.

In the garden

Regardless of the size of dog you have chosen, the garden should be securely fenced. The height of the fencing obviously depends on how big your dog will be, but bear in mind, some breeds are surprisingly agile and can clear a five-bar gate with ease.

There are also the 'tunnelers', who will find the smallest gap in the fencing to dig an escape route. Check the fastenings on all gates leading from your garden. If you have a pond or a swimming pool, make sure it is covered, or fenced off, so it is completely out of bounds. Tragically, many puppies have lost their lives through accidental drowning.

If you have a garden shed, make sure it is secured as substances such as insecticides are highly toxic. You will also need to make sure that all materials you use on the garden are pet friendly. There are a number of garden plants that are toxic to dogs; check the internet for a comprehensive list.

Buying equipment

You do not have to spend a fortune on equipment but there are a few essentials, which you should buy in advance.

Indoor crate

This is an invaluable piece of equipment which will provide a safe haven for your pup at times when you are not there to supervise. It is a place for your pup to rest, and to sleep in overnight – it should never be used as a means of punishment. If you plan to continue using a crate when your pup is fully grown, make sure you buy a crate that will be big enough to accommodate him.

Bedding

You will need at least two pieces of synthetic, fleece bedding – one to use while the other is being washed. This type of bedding is warm and cosy, it is machine washable and easy to dry.

Bowls

You will need two bowls – one for food and one for water. The best type to buy are those made of stainless steel which are easy to clean and virtually indestructible.

Collar and lead

To begin with, buy a soft, lightweight collar that can be adjusted as your puppy grows. Make sure the lead you buy has a secure trigger fastening.

Toys

You will be amazed at the range of toys designed for dogs and puppies. You can take your pick, but check that the toys are strong enough to resist chewing.

Arriving home

In the first few weeks of life, your puppy will have become accustomed to the safety and security of his breeder's home. He will have been nurtured by his mother and surrounded by his littermates, eating with them, playing with them, and sleeping with them.

The day you collect your puppy, everything will change. He will be placed in completely alien surroundings with people he does not know, and without the support of his mother and siblings. It is no wonder even the boldest puppy finds it quite a daunting experience.

Try to make the transition as smooth as possible by not overwhelming your puppy with too much attention. Allow him to explore his new surroundings – first the garden, then the room where you have located his crate – and give him a chance to find his feet.

Meeting the family

If you have children, they will be hugely excited by the new arrival so you will need to keep them calm. Allow each child to meet the puppy; if they are small, it is better if they sit on the floor as it is all too easy to drop a wriggly puppy. Each child can offer the puppy a small treat, making sure he takes it gently without biting or mouthing.

It is important that your children understand the golden rules of living with a puppy:

- A puppy must never be teased or played with roughly.

- If a puppy is eating or sleeping, he must not be disturbed.

- There must be no running, shouting or screaming when playing with a puppy.

- Games should involve the puppy's toys only – not the children's toys.

Initially, it is best to supervise all interactions between puppy and children to ensure that relations get off to a good footing. If a sense of mutual respect is established, they will soon become the best of friends.

Mouthing

One of the most common problems encountered when introducing a puppy to a family with small children is mouthing. A pup investigates everything with his mouth, and when he is playing with his littermates, he mouths, nips and bites. This is natural behaviour with other dogs, but it is not appropriate with people.

A puppy has to learn to inhibit his bite when he is being handled, or when he is playing with both children and adults. The puppies' mother will start to teach them – if a pup is playing rough and bites her, she will give a warning growl. In the same way, a pup will yelp if he is nipped by one of his littermates. This is seen as a signal and the pup knows he must stop.

In the family circle, you and your children must continue these lessons. If a pup attempts to mouth or nip, give a sharp cry, which will stop him in his tracks. You must then teach him to play without mouthing. This can be done using a treat:

- Show your puppy you have a treat and then place it in your closed fist.

- To begin with the pup will try to get the treat by pawing and mouthing your fist. When he finds this strategy is not working, he will stop mouthing and sit and think what to do next.

- At this instant, open your fist and let him have the treat.

- Keep practicing so your pup understands that when he does not mouth or nip, he gets a reward.

- Introduce the cue "gently" so your pup will replicate the desired behaviour in other situations such as when you are playing with a toy, or when he is being handled.

The resident dog

If you already have a dog, you will be anxious to
ensure the newcomer is accepted and your adult dog
does not feel jealous. The best plan is to introduce
the adult and the pup in the garden where there is
more space, and the adult will not feel his territory
has been invaded.

If your adult is boisterous, put him on a lead to start
with so the puppy is not, literally, bowled over. But
keep him on a loose lead, as you want him to behave
naturally rather than being controlled. In most
cases, it is best to interfere as little as possible and
allow the two dogs the opportunity to work out their
own relationship. Give the adult lots of praise and
encouragement when he is being friendly, but do not
get alarmed if he gives a warning growl. This is dog
communicating to dog, and the pup must learn to
respect his elder.

There are a few points to bear in mind while the two dogs are learning to live with each other:

- Do not feed the two dogs together until relations are well established.

- Do not leave the two dogs alone together (unless the pup is in a crate) as you are not there to intervene if there is a disagreement.

- If you having a game with toys, play with one dog at a time to prevent attempts to grab or steal toys from each other.

- Make sure your adult dog enjoys some quality time with you – such as going out for a walk – so he still feels special.

Introducing the cat

There is no reason why dogs and cats have to be sworn enemies – in fact, if you are tactful with initial interactions, they may learn to like each other!

- Hold your puppy in your lap and allow the cat to come up and sniff. Make sure the pup does not lunge at the cat.

- Distract the puppy with a toy or a treat and praise and reward him when he switches his attention away from the cat.

- Keep practicing so the puppy is more interested in the rewards you are offering than in the cat.

- Next, allow the puppy on the floor but make sure the cat has an escape route, such as a high surface, so he can get out of the way if he feels threatened. Allow the pup to look at the cat, and then call him away, offering him a toy or a treat.

- Supervise all interactions over the first few weeks so that both the puppy and the cat are familiar with each other. In time, the novelty will wear off and they will learn to live in harmony.

Mealtimes

If you have collected your puppy at eight weeks of age, he will probably be in a routine of getting four meals a day. In most cases, the breeder will give you a quantity of the food he is used to, which should last you for the first few days.

It is very important to stick to the same food and the same mealtimes, at least to begin with. A puppy has so much to get used to as he adapts to his new home, there is no point in risking a stomach upset by changing his diet as well.

If you decide to change his diet, do so gradually over a period of several days. Add a little of the new food to begin with, increasing the amount, meal by meal, until you have made a complete changeover.

Remember to keep a bowl of fresh drinking water available at all times.

Do not worry if your pup loses his appetite to begin with. It could well be that he is so preoccupied with his new surroundings that he cannot concentrate on his food. He will also miss the rivalry of feeding with his littermates.

Give your pup around 10 minutes to eat his food and if he loses interest and walks away, simply pick up the bowl and give him fresh food at his next meal. It will not be long before your pup is cleaning his bowl with relish! However, if you have any concerns, consult your vet.

Obviously the amount you feed will depend on the breed and the size. The breeder will be able to advise you on this. In fact, most breeders will give you a diet sheet, with details of a suggested feeding regime from puppyhood to adulthood.

As a general rule, meals are reduced from four a day to three at 12 weeks, and by six months, you will be feeding two meals a day. Some owners prefer to continue with this regime throughout their dog's life, others prefer to feed one larger meal a day.

Choosing
a diet

There are so many dog foods on offer in supermarkets and pet stores, it can be difficult to know what is best for your dog. Basically, there are three diets to choose from:

Complete

This is a dry diet specially manufactured to include all the nutrients your dog will need. It can be fed soaked or dry, but if you opt for feeding dry you must ensure your dog has plenty of drinking water available. This is easy and convenient to feed, and is popular among many dog owners. You can also select a diet to suit your dog's age and lifestyle, and there are even prescription diets for specific health issues.

Canned

Most dogs seem to find canned food very appetising; it is usually fed with hard biscuit, which also helps to keep teeth clean. Bear in mind that canned food has a high moisture content so check the ingredients listed on the label to ensure it has all the nutrients your dog needs.

B.A.R.F

This stands for Biologically Appropriate Raw Food and it consists of raw meat, bones, skin and vegetables– the type of diet eaten by our dogs' ancestors. This natural method of feeding is believed by some to be of benefit to a dog's all round health. If you are interested in feeding a Barf diet, you can buy the raw ingredients or you can order a Barf diet from a stockist listed on the internet.

If you are a first-time owner, you would do well to seek advice from your puppy's breeder when deciding on the most suitable diet. The breeder will have had many years' experience feeding dogs, and will have specialist knowledge of what suits your chosen breed.

Dangers of obesity

Regardless of the size of breed, you must guard against allowing your dog to become overweight.

Dogs are great con artists and will look at you with melting eyes as if to say: "I haven't eaten for days...". Do not fall for this ruse; it does not take many extra treats before a dog starts to pile on the pounds. An overweight dog is lethargic and will not enjoy his exercise; he is prone to a range of health problems and his life expectancy is considerably shortened. It is your duty to keep your dog fit and lean so he can enjoy life to the full.

House training

House training

This is a big issue for all owners when a puppy first arrives in his new home – in fact, many people see it as a stumbling block to taking on a pup. In reality, it is not half as hard as it sounds, and if you put the work in during the first few weeks, you will be surprised at how quickly your puppy learns to be clean.

Before you bring your puppy home, allocate an area in the garden that he will use for toileting. If you take your pup to this place every time he needs to spend, he will understand what you want him to do. It also helps when you pick up after your pup, particularly if you have young children and need to keep the garden scrupulously clean.

The key to successful house training is establishing a routine. Take your puppy out at the following times:

- When he wakes in the morning.

- After every meal.

- After a play session.

- When he wakes up after a snooze.

- Last thing at night.

A small puppy has to relieve himself at frequent intervals, so you should never leave him longer than two hours during the day before taking him to his toileting area.

It is tempting to leave a puppy to relieve himself on his own – particularly if it is cold or raining. However, this short cut will not pay dividends. You need to stay with your pup and when he spends give a verbal cue, such as "busy" or "be clean", so that he learns to associate the word with the action. When he performs, praise him lavishly.

Do not make the mistake of rushing back inside as soon as your puppy has relieved himself. From your pup's point of view, he will think that as soon as he spends, he is taken out of the garden, which is full of interesting scents and places to explore. He may decide to employ delaying tactics next time you take him outside in order to prolong his time in the garden.

As soon as he has spent, play with him for a couple of minutes, or run through a couple of easy training exercises so he can enjoy some one-on-one time with you before going back into the house.

If you stick to the routine outlined above, your puppy will soon get the hang of house training, but bear in mind that you will need to do the thinking for him – taking him out at the prescribed times – until he is at least six months old.

When accidents happen

It is inevitable that your puppy will have the occasional accident while he is being house trained. In most cases, the fault will be yours – you left him too long between trips out to the garden, or you did not whisked him outside the moment he awoke.

Do not blame yourself, but more importantly, do not get cross with your puppy. If you find a mess, simply clean it up, making sure you use a deodoriser so he is not tempted to spend in the same place again. There is no point in scolding your puppy after the event, he will not associate the telling off with what he has done, and you will only confuse him.

If you catch your puppy red-handed, pick him up, take him out to his toileting area and give him the verbal cue you have taught him. If he obliges, remember to give lots of praise.

Puppies tend to give warning signals before they spend, so be on the alert if you see your pup sniffing or circling when he is in the house. Take him outside without delay.

Settling in

A puppy has a lot to get used to when he arrives in his new home, but with your help and support he will soon feel safe and secure. However, the first few nights are likely to be trying for you both.

If you see a litter of puppies in the nest, they will lie in one big heap, getting warmth and comfort from each other's bodies. When a pup leaves the breeder's home, he is going to have to cope with nights on his own.

An indoor crate is invaluable in this situation as your pup can be confined in a safe place where he cannot harm himself – even though he can still make a lot of noise.

Make the crate cosy with bedding in the back half and newspaper in the front half. This means that if your pup needs to spend overnight – and most pups cannot last all night long to begin with – he does not have to soil his bedding.

Take the following steps before you put your pup in his crate:

- Feed your pup a couple of hours beforehand so he has a chance to spend before being crated, but he will still feel reasonably full and content.

- Have a play session with your pup in an attempt to tire him out.

- Take him to his toileting area last thing at night.

- Put him in his crate with a small biscuit to tempt him in.

Some owners recommend putting a soft toy in the crate so the puppy can snuggle up to it, but you must be certain that he cannot chew bits out of it. You can put a ticking clock near the crate or leave the radio playing, which may help the pup to settle.

The vast majority of puppies do put up a pretty vocal protest – some keep it up for half an hour or so, others have a lot more stamina. The problem is that if you go to your puppy to comfort him, he will cry every time he goes in his crate as he knows you will come running. In the long run, it is best to ignore him so that he learns to settle. In most cases, a pup will understand that he goes into his crate to rest, and will stop protesting.

If you really cannot stand your puppy's cries, or if you are worried that he is disturbing the neighbours, you can set up the crate by your bedside for the first few nights. You can then move it to a permanent location, such as the kitchen or utility room, when the pup is more settled.

Remember that it is important for a puppy to learn to cope on his own for short periods. If you are constantly with him, he may become anxious if a situation arises when he has to spend time on his own. He may bark and whine, and in a worst-case scenario, he may become so upset that he defecates, or becomes destructive.

If your puppy accepts the crate as his own cosy den, he will be perfectly happy to spend time away from you, and problems with separation anxiety need never arise.

Socialising your puppy

How a puppy develops depends on his breed, his individual genetic make-up, and on his environment. The role you play in nurturing your puppy is of vital importance and it will have enormous influence on the way he behaves for the rest of his life.

A puppy needs to understand and accept the world he lives in so that he is calm and confident in all situations he encounters. Some pups may be braver than others, but if you expose your puppy to different sights and sounds and allow him to meet a variety of different people and different animals, he will develop the skills to cope without feeling fearful or threatened.

In the first few weeks of arriving in his new home, allow your pup to have the following experiences, making sure they are always positive so that he grows in confidence:

- Introduce him to household equipment, such as the washing machine and the vacuum cleaner.

- If you do not have children, arrange to meet some, making sure all interactions are carefully supervised.

- Accustom your pup to meeting visitors to the house – particularly people who may be wearing uniform or carting unfamiliar equipment.

- If you do not have a dog at home, arrange for a dog of sound temperament that is fully vaccinated to come and visit.

- Take your pup out in the car for short outings.

- You will have to wait until your puppy is fully vaccinated before he can walk on the lead outside your home. But you can carry him along a quiet road so that he gets used to traffic, and to meeting passers-by who will want to give him a stroke.

When your puppy has completed his course of vaccinations, you can broaden his experiences over the next few months so that he receives a comprehensive education that will equip him for adult life. Here are some ideas for socialising your pup:

- Go for a walk in a quiet neighbourhood so your pup gets used to seeing traffic at ground level.

- If your puppy is coping well, go to busier places where there is heavy traffic and crowds of people.

- Go to an outdoor event, such as a car-boot sale or an open-air market where they will be hustle and bustle from stallholders and shoppers, as well as lots of interesting scents.

- Take your pup for a walk in your local park; go past the children's play area so he can hear the sound of children playing, and if you have practised your recall you can let him off the lead so he can meet some other dogs.

- Go to a railway station and walk along the platform so your pup can get used to the sound of trains and also to loudspeaker announcements.

First lessons

It is never too soon to start training your puppy – it is much easier to establish the behaviour you want rather than trying to break bad habits.

Start by finding a reward that your puppy values; this could be a food treat, or some pups are motivated by playing with a toy. In order to train a puppy successfully, he must have a reward that is worth working for.

In the following exercises, a treat is used as a lure and a reward, but a toy can be used in exactly the same way.

Sit

This is an easy exercise to teach and your puppy will pick it up in no time. Hold a treat just above his head and as he looks up at it, he will lower his hindquarters and sit. Practice this a few times, and then add the verbal cue, "Sit".

Down

Start with your pup in a sit, and lower a treat towards
the floor. Your pup will go down to try to reach it,
first with his front and then the back end will follow.
Again, add the verbal cue, "Down" when your puppy
understands what you want him to do.

Walking on a lead

This is a case of practice makes perfect. Start by attaching a lead and allow your pup to wander, making sure the lead does not get caught up. Then take hold of the lead and follow the pup, allowing him to choose where he wants to go. The next step is to encourage your pup to walk with you. You can encourage him by holding a treat in your hand and when he has walked a few steps at your side, following the treat, stop and reward him. Build this up gradually, introducing circles and changes of direction. Do not progress too quickly; it is far better to have a short stretch of good heelwork where your puppy is co-operating, rather than letting the lesson become a chore.

Stay

It is easiest to teach this exercise with your puppy on lead so you can control him. Start by asking him to "Sit" and then stepping one pace to the side. Go back and praise him for staying in position. Repeat on the other side, and then stand in front of him and try stepping back a couple of paces before returning to him. If he is staying in position, introduce the verbal cue, "Stay". Build this up gradually, extending the distance and the amount of time you can leave your puppy.

In conclusion

As you have discovered, there is a lot of hard work involved in taking on a puppy. You need to do your research carefully so you choose a breed to suit your lifestyle; you will also need to find out about the special care he needs in terms of diet, grooming, exercise and health care. Then, when a puppy becomes part of your family you must find time to train him and socialise him.

There is no doubt that bringing a puppy into your life is a huge undertaking but you will be rewarded a thousand fold by the love, loyalty – and entertainment – you will get from your beloved canine companion.

My puppy's
details

My puppy's name: ....

Current weight: ....

Date of birth: ....

Breed: ....

Colouration: ....

Vaccination shedule: ....

....

....